Mama's Got a Dog!

Life and Time on the Old Valdosta Road

(a book for children of all ages)

by Donald (Donny) N. Roberson, Jr.

RoseDog🐾Books

PITTSBURGH, PENNSYLVANIA 15238

RoseDog Books
585 Alpha Drive
Suite 103
Pittsburgh, PA 15238
Visit our website at www.rosedogbookstore.com

ISBN: 978-1-6442-6697-7
eISBN: 978-1-6442-6720-2

Author – Donald (Donny) N. Roberson, Jr.

10538 Old Valdosta Road

Nashville, GA 31639

dnrobersonjr@gmail.com

Sketches by Avery Barnett.

Pictures were taken by children of Idelle Roberson.

Chapter One

Way back when, we had a few dogs, they were 'outside' dogs. They were ours, but they were on their own, there was no collar, no going to the "vet" (veterinarian). We fed them, we played with them, and they knew they belonged to us, but they slept where they wanted and wandered where they wanted.

One of the first dogs I can remember was named "Midnight." She was a short small dog with long curly black hair. She had one litter and there were puppies running around which was a lot of fun.

There was "Boss" – with amazing curly off white fur. He was famous for running around in circles as he would chase a car. It was like he was chasing his own tail. People even drove out to our house on purpose to watch him.

All of these dogs brought us love and added to our fun outside. It was normal to have a dog at the house. Everyone usually had a dog outside in their yard, not in their house.

Chapter Two

There were four of us children at home.

Pa was busy at his work. He was trying to sell tractors.

And Ma was busy at home and in the community. She got the idea for us to have a 'pure bred' dog. She decided on a boxer. He had a real official name – von George of Mason. George was the first dog allowed in the house, but only a few rooms, and he still slept outside. He was a lot of fun and full of energy.

He was an outside dog, with a pedigree, and he was happy there, we loved him. He was very handsome. We learned about how certain dogs will get their ears and tail clipped.

My job was to feed George every morning, I still do not like the smell of canned dog food. In order to add to the dog food, Mama would sometimes cook an egg, and pour bacon grease over all of that. No wonder he was so happy! She said, "that would make his coat shine."

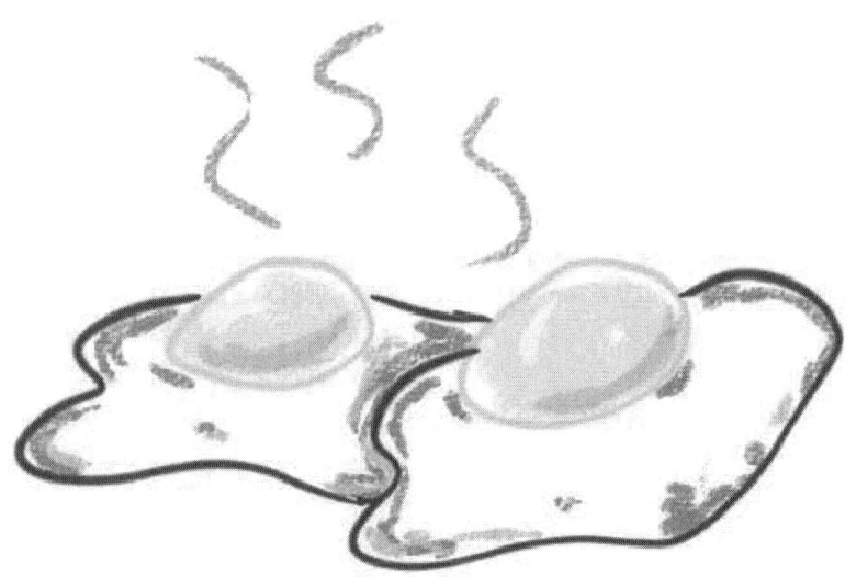

One sad day he was hit by a car on the road in front of our house.

We got another boxer and also named him George, Junior – and called him Junior.

There was "Duke" – a handsome mixture between an Irish setter and a Golden Labrador. During this time I would often go for a jog for three miles. He would always run about 20 yards in front of me. Later in his life, he started to sneak off at night and catch chickens from a farm about half a mile away. Someone noticed Duke was covered with ticks from running in the woods, Ma banished him to stay at the 'shop.' The shop was our name for Daddy's business.

This was a farm equipment business. Duke really enjoyed being out there, and all of the farmers enjoyed petting him. Interesting how quickly dogs adapt to new situations.

Duke was the last dog for a long while.

Chapter Three

Many years later, Daddy began to have trouble breathing.

His lungs were not working right.

There was not a cure for this, and soon it was too much for him, and he died.

Daddy had grown up on the farm, and there were also dogs. He would often make funny comments about one of our dogs. Seeing how they would always stay out of the sun, as opposed to us, "son, see how smart they are."

Chapter Four

Mama was alone at home for the first time in her life. One thing that helped her feel safe was getting a 'security system' in her home.

It took a while and eventually the sadness and emptiness of losing a life partner left after 2 or 3 years. She began to resume her life again, but she was sort of lonely at home.

She continued her many activities such as taekwondo, golf, biking, bridge, and getting involved again in the community through the church and some volunteer activities.

And still, there was this empty house, before there was always someone to talk to.

She had lots of friends, was involved in many activities, and even dated a few different men.

Chapter Five

South Georgia is a semi-tropical area; it's very warm and hot, in the spring and summer. There is often humidity in the air of 90 – 100%.

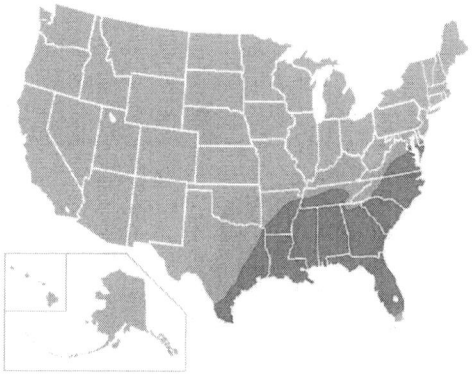

This atmosphere is host to varieties of plants, birds, lizards, snakes, even alligators. Sometimes a turtle would venture across our yard and the dog at home would have lots of fun barking or playing with the turtle, but he was no match for the turtle's hard shell. Lizards of all sorts were everywhere, bugs, mosquitos, gnats, and all sorts of critters.

One bright sunny day Mary Payne (the only neighbor) called Ma on the telephone. "Idelle there is an alligator coming across the ditch to your yard." Ma goes outside to check on everything. Sure enough a large alligator about 6 – 7 feet was slowly moving toward her house! The yard has lots of straw in the flower beds and the gator went to one section of the flower bed and got under a bunch of straw to cool off.

There was a lot of excitement. They called the game warden – they bring a truck and remove the alligator to a better place for him and ma.

Chapter Six

Mama loved to sit outside on her back porch. A long narrow porch. If the weather was good she would sit all day, and read the newspaper, or look at other things.

One day a dog wandered up. She looked closer and he had blood all over him. She did not know what to do. She shooed him away.

Chapter Seven

I suggested a few times she should get a dog. She always said, no, it would be too much trouble.

One summer, when I was going to be home, I thought I would just go and get a dog for her. And if it did not work out, I would take him/her back. She said no.

Later that same summer, I left to check on my house in another town for a few days.

During this time, Ma opened the front door and there was a small little puppy. She sees this pitiful, small puppy crawling toward her, she runs in the house and closes the door.

He never left.

She decided she would give him something to eat.

When I returned from my trip, mama said, "I see the surprise you left." I did not know what she was talking about. Then around the corner comes this little beautiful puppy bouncing, wagging, and joyful with life. He looked maybe like a mixture of something, we often say Heinz 57. I was shocked there was a dog at the house and Ma seemed to enjoy it.

He was so cute, so active, and playful.

Ma and Red on the back porch.

He would sleep in the garage, on a blanket we had, and we would shut the door to keep him safe.

Mother and I left for a previously planned trip to Atlanta. We were going to do a few things, go to the Fox theatre and Zoo, and visit with her grandchildren. We left him some food, and we drove away. Ma said if he is here when we get back, I will keep him.

Three days later, after the fun time in Atlanta, I had remembered mother's words, as we slowly drove into the garage, I was wondering...and sure enough, he comes bounding around the corner.

I said, "OK, Mama you got to name him."

Later, she said, I am going to name him Red, after your daddy's nickname in college.

Chapter 8

Red was ma's first dog. We had those others, which I told you about, but they were ours, this one really became hers. She got more serious about Red, and fixed up a little blanket, even heater, in the garage. And we would close the door to the garage at night so he could not get out.

Red Roberson after his operation (neutered).

He was so cute he would jump and play and seemed so happy, and he would chase balls, and bounce after them. Ma liked to buy him a toy, Red was so happy with them, and he would often dig a hole and bury them. He enjoyed digging holes! For us it was almost a shock – 'did you know – Mama's got a dog!'.

Before she was focused on golf, or church, or family, or her house, or something she was doing in the yard. Now she became focused on this cute bundle of joy.

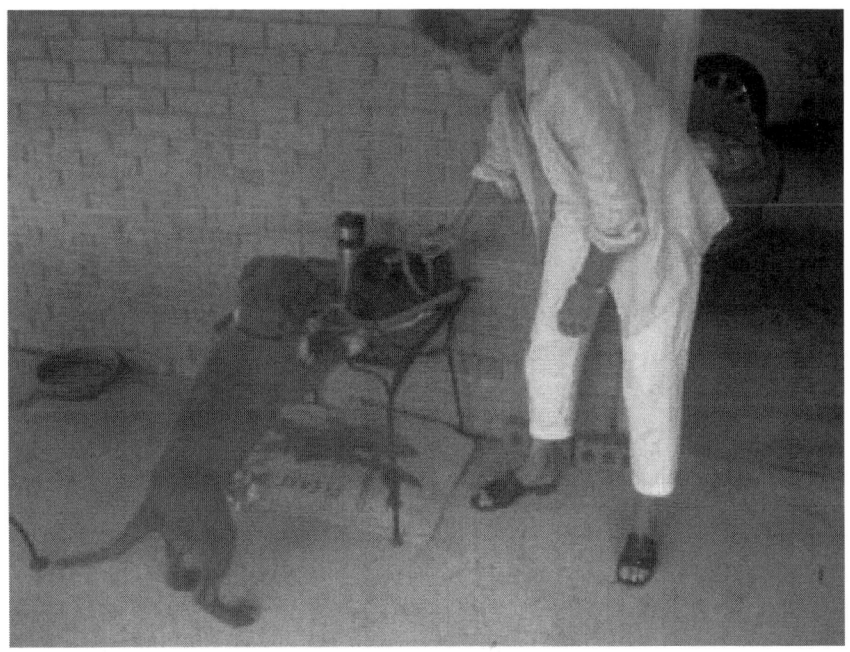

Ma trying to keep Red away from her pocketbook.

He would often 'paw' on your legs, and this resulted in many scratches on ma's leg. Ma takes him to the vet for a checkup, and has him neutered.

Taking Red for a walk – Dogwood Street, Nashville, GA.

Sam my brother has been a dog owner for much longer, and he would often give advice. 'Get a crate, and keep him in the crate, or train him using the crate. Get a shock collar so he can have the boundary of the yard.' This electric collar, seemed very involved, it came with long pages of detail of what to do to train the dog. I was thinking that he would sort of self-train. He did get shocked a few times, we put up some flags, as boundaries. So, we did not know what we were doing. We were hoping he was trained, but he was not.

Red was very playful and fun to watch. He brought a lot of fun to mother's life.

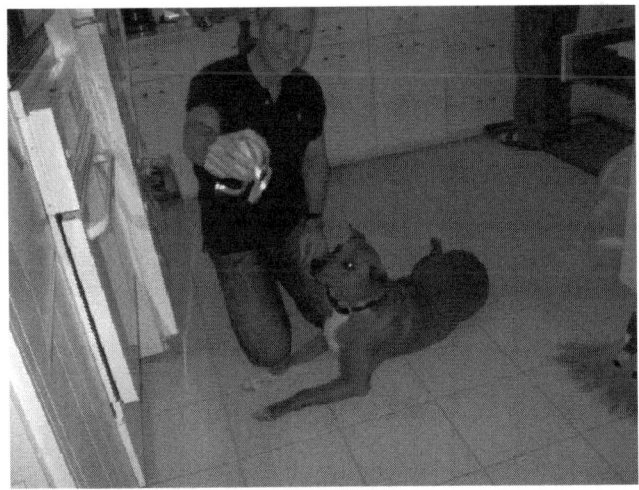

Sam and Red on the kitchen floor.

Chapter 9

Mama took the electric collar off of him at night, and he was still sleeping in the garage. One night, for some reason the garage door was open, and Red went out into the early morning to investigate something.

That was his last adventure. He never came back. He was found on the road, some car had hit him. Surprisingly his body was not torn, or any blood. But he was dead. Someone recognized Red and brought him to mother. She was devastated and cried a lot. She had the man to lay him in the back flower bed under a tree. He is buried in her flower bed.

Mother wrote some things about this experience with Red.

"It has been over four weeks since the unthinkable happened...Never did I ever think of something happening like on March 19, never, never, never. We were beginning to understand each other better, and he had become a habit that I liked. Had thought he was safe...Red you have a ball in backyard, and one in the kitchen, I have not moved them, you left memories everywhere, when I would drive in, I would look all over the yard to see where you would be, I miss you."

She was sad for a while, she cried a lot, and told everyone about Red.

Chapter 10

The next summer I was home for a while and I suggested to ma, let's try another dog. We had gotten a crate for him to stay. We found a dog over the internet, and ma liked his color. Ma wanted the dog to match the inside of her house. ☺

We drove to an animal shelter in Vienna, Ga. The lady in charge had a hard time getting him out to visit us. (I should have known that was not a good sign.) He was hiding under a car. She finally coaxed him out, we put a leash on him, and ma walked a bit with him. And we thought this dog will be ok. She decided she would get him, she paid a fee, and they were going to neuter him. We would pick him up in one week.

Ma and Ritch on the back porch.

Ma named him Ritch, which is her family name or her mother's maiden name. After one week, we drove and picked him up. He was not a happy dog. I don't think I ever saw him wag his tail. And worse, he would not even come for a treat. Ma was real patient and she would walk with him about the yard, and we would put him in the crate for sleeping. Ma was walking with him, and I would try to play with him. However, he was not really responsive, or attentive to us. Ma would try to give him a treat and he would not even come. After three weeks of this, I said, ma, this Ritch is not working out, I am sorry, but he is just not worth your time and effort. So, we reluctantly agreed, we called the lady, she was also disappointed, but we agreed to bring him back the next day.

We live in a rural area outside of the town, and there was a dead deer in the ditch across from our house. It looked terrible, there were buzzards around, and there was a bad smell. We were outside with Ritch and somehow he smells this and takes off running. We had no idea where he was or where he went. I just told ma to relax, he will come back, or he is gone. In about an hour he returns, it is already dark, we were relieved and let him inside. To our shock, he smelled like dead deer, and he was completely covered in the rotten carcass of that poor dead animal. He was running through her spotless and beautiful home covered in that mess.

I finally get the leash on him, and get him outside. Ritch was scared of me, but mother very patiently washed the filth off of him out on the back porch. We get him in the crate, and during the night I can hear him coughing and gagging. I realize, he has eaten this rotten animal and will begin to vomit, or even worse die. It was very late, I put ear plugs in my ear, and try to get some sleep.

The next morning his crate is covered in some vile black

vomit. I get him outside with a leash and tie him up. We now take him to the veterinarian and let them wash him. Ma gets him, and drives him back to his dog shelter. I wonder whatever happened to Ritch. I wonder what made him such a sad dog.

Chapter 11

About three weeks later, I suggest to ma let's just go look at an official dog shelter in Valdosta to see if we can find another one. We were already in Valdosta and near the place, so we go, and talk to the people.

We talk to them and they invite us to look. Amazing we found a lab like dog, with a tan and beige color that ma likes. They tell us to go in a special waiting room. They bring in this dog with the tan color coat. And, unlike the other one, his tail is wagging, he is looking at us in a friendly way. I clap my hands and he willingly comes to me. He was friendly and loving to ma. We decided to try him. Ma was already sure, she paid for him to be neutered. We would pick him up in a week!

Chapter Thirteen

Mama's got a dog! We decided to also call him Ritch, since the name meant so much to ma. Ma took this dog seriously and the first thing was to train him with an electrical collar. Elijah, a man who has helped ma around the house was a big help. It is a radar electrical collar. And Ritch seemed to be okay. This was one of the main misunderstandings with Red. Ma had bought him an electrical collar, and I tried to help with this training of Red and eventually the first Ritch. But, it was much more work than I had anticipated. And they were not correctly trained, however, Ma thought they were.

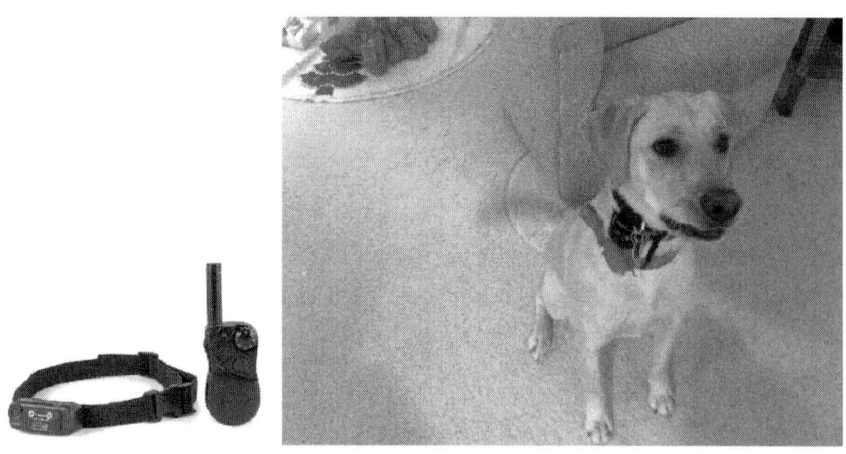

Young Ritch in the house. Ritch Roberson

In addition to the electrical collar. She enrolled in classes for dog training. She bought him a fancy bed and put it next to her bed. She also bought a special blanket for the car so he could ride in the back seat without messing up the car too much. My brother got her some fancy feeding trough that was elevated. This dog has gone from animal shelter to dog heaven!

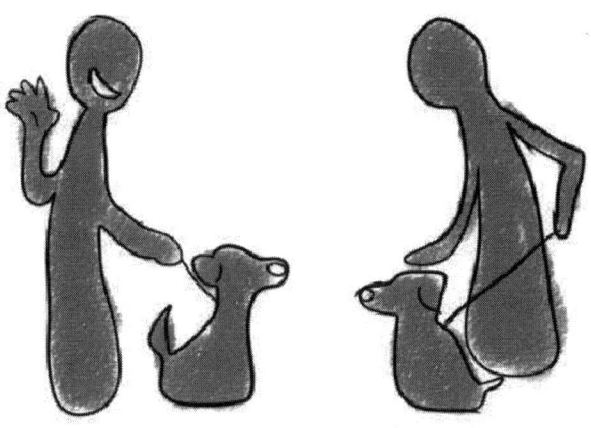

She enjoyed teaching Ritch tricks. She even taught him to get the paper. Ritch loved to run about the house – he was protecting Mas's boundary. Eventually he even wore a path down in the grass. He would ride with her in the car. Often she would cuddle with him, and scratch his stomach. He became a companion and protector for her.

Ma trying to teach Ritch some trick. (She taught him to get the paper, roll over, and shake your hand.)

Ma loved sitting on the back porch, just reading the paper, looking at magazines, just sitting there, and listening to the birds. Ritch would come up, and put his nose under her arm.

They were both happy.

Chapter Fourteen

There were a few problems with Ritch.

Even with the electrical collar on; he ran away a few times.

Ma would try to find him, and would go on the street and even stop people to ask her to find him!

He had to be retrained with the electrical collar. Thank you Elijah.

He enjoyed digging holes and digging up the shrubbery!

When the irrigation came on he loved to bite the nozzles of the irrigation.

Chapter Fifteen

Mama got a dog!

He would sleep in her room, sometimes on her bed, and then mainly on his own bed.

He rode with her in her car. Everyone began to recognize them together. Among some of the 'drive- thrus' in Nashville; they would even offer Ritch a treat.

She would often take him to dog training school. He had a special red mat where he sat, and waited for her commands.

Many times especially in the mornings, ma would get on the floor and do some stretching, and then she would always cuddle with Ritch.

And sometimes I would be 'rough' with him, especially if he was trying to eat out of her hands, or I thought take advantage of her. I would scold him, and she would say, 'Donny don't you talk to Ritch that way!!!'

Ma had a special place for his things in the house.

Chapter 16

I wish I could say – and 'they lived happily ever after.' Those sorts of 'fairy tales' exist only in some rare situations. Ma showed all of us about life – from this special relationship with Ritch. Earlier she would have never had time for such – she was busy, raising four children, involved in the community, and then on her own, developing many activities from golf, to taekwondo, to bridge. It was toward the end of her life, when she allowed a dog to enter her life. He became a real companion for her and now we will show you some great pictures of this time!

*Ma with Trek, Sam's
first Great Dane.*

*Ritch, I am too busy on my phone
to play with you!*

Ma with Buddy, Fonda
(my sister's dog) and Stacy.

Sam and Ma, Sam and Ted
now have two great danes
and two cats!

Ma and Ritch
all dressed up.

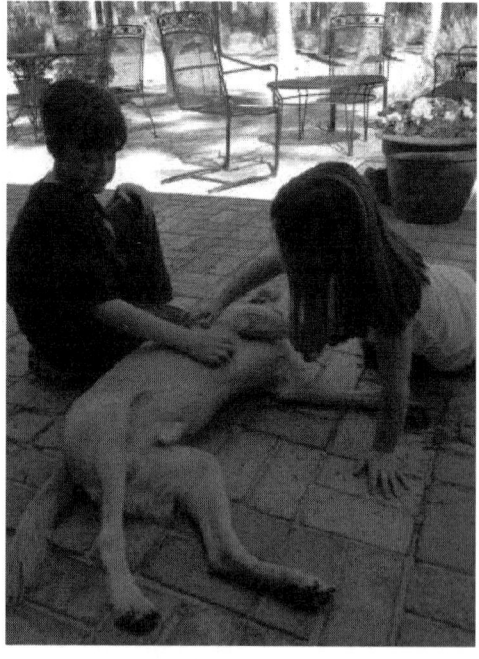

bo and kate – mothers great
grandchildren playing with ritch

Everyone in the family has dogs,
here is sister Linda with her dog.

Ritch playing with his
Christmas stocking.

Back Page Information

The author, Donald (Donny) N. Roberson, Jr. is also a son of this dog owner. Roberson is currently Associate Professor at Palacky University in the Czech Republic. He has also has worked with college students with one Christian student organization called CRU. Although growing up in south Georgia he has lived all over the USA as well as several years in central Europe, mainly Croatia and Czech Republic. His research interest involves personal education, aging, physical activity, travel and tourism. He resides mainly in Berrien County, Nashville, Georgia.

This book for all ages offers a glimpse into the wide and interesting life of my mother. She showed us how to live life when one is older, embracing new adventures, and laying others aside. She showed us how an animal could add a new dimension to one's life. She loved being around people, yet she would have never written a book about her life, this was a story I thought would encourage many of you. Although she has left us now, Ritch is still here, and you can come and play with him!